Elegies

Shearsman Library Vol. 10

Elegies

Harry Guest

Shearsman Library

Second Edition.
Published in the United Kingdom in 2018 by
Shearsman Library
an imprint of Shearsman Books
by Shearsman Books Ltd
50 Westons Hill Drive
Emersons Green
BRISTOL
BS16 7DF

Shearsman Books Ltd Registered Office
30–31 St. James Place, Mangotsfield, Bristol BS16 9JB
(this address not for correspondence)

www.shearsman.com

ISBN 978-1-84861-596-0

Elegies was first published by Pig Press, Durham, in 1980.
The sequence was subsequently collected in the author's
A Puzzling Harvest: Collected Poems 1955–2000,
(London: Anvil Press Poetry, 2002).

Reprinted here by kind permission of Carcanet Press, Manchester,
for Anvil Press Poetry; http://www.carcanet.co.uk/cgi-bin/
indexer?product=9780856463549.

Contents

The First Elegy

The area was overgrown. Brambles and fireweed
had to be uprooted before a boundary
was agreed upon and the last pale
driven in next to the first. Sometimes
the acreage is complete before pen touches paper,
at others the map only remains itself and the final
shading contradicts the outline made at the start,
for example a grey summer's day and on the lake
hardly waves only the slightest folding
over of water on water with nothing reflected
though the hills enclosing it were purple
and on three sides trees came down to the shore.
Adults were elsewhere. We skimmed stones or sat round
in the gritty boat-house. What furniture I remember
appears scoured and cheap. There was a gramophone
playing swing. Unheard mosquitoes
stung our bare legs. Today we stroll beneath lime-trees
in another garden that does not belong to us.
At that time we could not have known each other
even though in a sense sharing the same time-zone,
privation, absence of sunlight, for war
had removed our fathers. The faces are unlabelled,
those melodies possess only a period texture.
I cannot recall who owned the property nor where
we went later. There was a small rocky island
but no boat and I couldn't swim in those days.
The dramatis personae were children on their own
for an afternoon and you and I increasingly
find ourselves left behind as they run over stubble

where the last swallows flash or enter gloomy
chambers in some ruined castle where the lintels
are too low for our foreheads. But a chipped stone egg
on my desk admonishes me for change
emerges from the air and colours the thinnest
depictions of the past. Late June there. Few flowers –
the one rhododendron flecked with unclenched scarlet
shows by its listlessness it has fulfilled
a yearly duty. The blinds are half drawn though only
on one far field where the hay has been cut
sunlight, slanting, picks out yellow among the green.
Knowledge of being alive at a given moment –
given if not taken – has details of heat and shrubbery
absorbing the past tense before we exclude them.
On the ground floor, there in the room forming the corner,
two oil-paintings, each about the size of a postcard,
display these illusions: one, a path through a wood in spring,
the other, a slow stream broadening into pools
under brown foliage. Both show what was needed
though neither comments on anything here
since the brush-strokes limit the scene not for the viewer
only but for the dead painter himself.
The way they've been hung would imply that it's the second
picture that holds autumn replacing April.
It could though be the other way around.
Take a day, any day, says the old fortune-teller.
It may be one that rises with indifference
to the surface, flicks the merest hint of a red
fin, gold scales, one among others, but at that time
you sat and read or went upstairs in a house
that has since been destroyed. You showed me the place,
now asphalt, near the church we were married in.

A copper beech spreads over this wall
and the dead elms show stark amid all the green.
When you were ascending that stair you saw
floor-boards stained dark, a carpeted edge of landing,
no foreshadow of a wind with dust and fumes
blowing across a sunken highway or its intrusion
years later into our talk. You stepped into space
going perhaps from one high room to another
and the crunch of gravel is cancelled under
our shoes as we leave this path for the lawn
but where I wonder will the two of us be when this
is remembered together or separately. The sun by now
has closed the last of the distant hay-fields though one
shaft of light sinks through green water in the estuary.
The open sea is concealed by the long shoulder
of the foreland. In theory you can walk round any lake.

The Second Elegy

Locality is present in the curve of a bowl
and the style has lost all heritage, all sense
of place, gone nameless, international.
Geology though cannot be flouted and subtler
changes happen in the quality of clay
even from village to village. The water, pigment,
wood-ash, flowing through space, reach time. It is hard
to detect lost sunlight or lines on the potter's hands
but soil round the roots of the plum-tree still
matters when fruit is eaten miles from the farm.
Some years ago now, on a walking holiday,
I encountered the whereabouts of a ghost.
At a threshold in the centre of the manor-house
you moved three centuries. The owner's voice
went on explaining but now there was a sweet
illness in my nostrils that got stronger
as we mounted the stairs till in the narrow
bathroom overwhelmed I had to lean on the cold wall
hearing words with difficulty through a smell
of rotten flowers, vase-water, meat going off,
and it was there according to the legend
that the dead monk had lain. There are also
the books to be chosen when one is about to cross
a desert. It is important to know something of the rocks
as well as the living things – rare blooms, the snake
coiled to strike – for there are bound to be lodestones.
Before selecting compass and penknife
one is strongly recommended to make a note
of one's own name and address, even mark the house

on the map for mirages occur and time-slips
and people have been known to stray far from the dusty
water-courses. No one belongs in an airport.
We motored over with rugs and a wicker
picnic-hamper to watch the fragile 'planes taxi
on the flat grass. Mechanics and travellers seemed
to have a place there but then that was an aerodrome.
We lay together at the foot of the slope discussing
desire in whispers, the dew was tracking the sun
as it diminished, the busy or languid players
cast distorted shadows on the field and the bat
struck the ball a full second before the sound reached us.
You watch lightning flicker over the tossing trees
and count five spaces of time as one mile. Today
the bar of twilight stretched between pole and pole
travels as fast but we adjust our watches
without winding them. Many have died since that time
and I have mourned them, attended the funeral,
grieved for the unseen smile, the dependable love,
but then dry seeds dropped in the earth give no
indication of stalk or flower, no glossy
berry or flourish of leaves, if a pun is not flippant
there is no hint of the yew-tree, indeed
looking at a corpse one would say, This is nothing.
The soul has begun its journey. You listen
to a record with the cat on your lap, the sounds
pass her unheeded. We also fail to intercept
movement of angels or the clamourous sense
made by the dead we knew. Other examples
demonstrate time – petrified sea-shells clinging
to the mountain-top, cold accumulations
of lava carved by the endless wind. A grouse

scuttled over the heather and I searched
for the nest without finding it. Unseen, always,
the wonder of speckled egg, of shrivelled leaf
and the seed-case is matched by the wonder
of fossil and rainbow. This is the interchange
of faith and belief. A sandstone escarpment
drops almost sheer to the north. Far below
in the green cup scooped by ice is a round pool
and sheep are grazing. In better weather
you could see more but at noon sudden spurts of rain
blur even the near-distance and grey shreds of cloud
pass level with the summit. It is politic
to keep out proper names as far as possible.
Poems aren't works of reference. They provide
the interested reader with the kit he needs
for an excursion into the uncharted hills
from which he'll come back tanned, unfocused, acquainted
with other ways of expressing each pavement or garden.
And there are as many editions of poems
as there are readers because *house*
will have a different shape for each of us
and *apple* a different taste. What do you see
when the word *red* is mentioned – bricks, a cock's comb,
the Whitsun altar, part of a flag, a judge's robes,
last Wednesday's sunset, blood at the dentist's, flamingoes,
garnets, a pillar box, fuchsia, morocco leather,
a pimpernel? What is selected will of course
isolate you for nobody includes the same
objects in a suitcase. Only music perhaps
can command the logic of its ingredients.
Wherever painting is involved the room,
the air dictate their gold, their mistiness. Glitter

of flood-water gets into the simplest paragraph
of a letter home so how can a poet say what is
or is not present in his poem. Fixing the terms
is the first task though organised with dangers
like opening windows on the cold side of a house.

The Third Elegy

Reality never gets into the newspapers.
A snapshot or a television programme
are most remarkable for what they leave out.
Swann said, 'They call our attention each day
to insignificant things whereas we read
three or four times in our life the books in which
lie the essentials.' Outlines of metaphor
rest on the map and the rain falling so quietly
is not the real rain. Water-lilies bloom now
in the pool, wax-yellow, scarlet. The dragonfly
we saw yesterday darts, a bronze flash among reeds,
and I stroll twice a day down to the post office
and collect nothing. None of this is correct
though the truth is present as a tight bead of water
among the hard petals. You took me by the hand
and told me of your unhappiness. No phrase,
no caress of mine reached the boundary of sadness,
altered it. This won't work either though reality
sometimes occurs in a poem just as it's only
in examination of time that eternity
makes any sense. If on a journey you stay
obsessed with the contents of your pockets
you will not be touched by the development of space
and space is the protection of the infinite.
The bird sang deep in the forest, the horseman
galloping up the ride did not hear its call
though later that evening when the rain held off
the crescents punched by the hooves brimmed with water
and perhaps the same bird went flying across

its own reflection. Wonder is a faculty
many do their utmost to smother in children
but when the pear drops on wet grass and the moon
urges the tide among salt-flats, the world
declares its magic the way in the silent garden
the figure walking by the tall box-hedge
was not there at the turn in the path. Two people
in love who share the same interests – films, coins, wine –
disagree over the method of pruning roses
and fascination with cut glass or prehistory
may appear uninviting. But poetry
is neither a pastime nor a public act.
It is an ordering and from that rearrangement
each reader extracts another. In among
the gestures of the orchestra a music emerges
that was not the composer's intention.
You can train the intellect as you would a retriever
or a sheep-dog but it is only one of many
apprehensions – there are also the five
senses, instinct a sixth one, emotions forming
a barrier like intolerance or else a dye
like joy, a soul that teaches us to love
and the spirit, atrophied in many, that holds
relations outside time. It is as absurd
to limit response to reason as to obey
a tone-deaf man's view of a concert.
I do not try hard enough to see through your eyes.
And I know, dear, I bore you. Once years ago
an archer entered the mews where dusty windows
brought in the morning and hooded falcons
gripped their perches. He chose ten arrows.
Dew glistened on the short grass for the hay

had been stacked the week before. He set the target
clear against the darkness of the forest.
Stringing his bow he shot the arrows one by one
which missed the padded circle and stuck like a grove
of leafless saplings bent by the wind. How else
can I define my love as the words employed
replace my passion with the unreal events
of metaphor? How may I leave my love for you
fixed on the fields of time if I can't
convey the unspoken except with words.
Others have painted the conquest of death and shown
the calm Christ stepping over the sprawled soldiers.
Others depicted the blaze of recognition in the inn
as the travellers grasp the fact they've been walking
along the edge of two worlds. Reality lies
in the empty tomb, on the road to Emmaus.
What will convince you that this is not blasphemy?
Love must go beyond the here and now
if it is to be anywhere. I think I tried
to read the misery in your eyes that day.
When you cross a familiar room in the darkness
the table you do not brush against is still there.

The Fourth Elegy

The starting-point may once have been a rose
or a rose-seed or, as you watch through glass
burnished by autumn, one petal falling
and striking the thorns as it falls. An age
of lyricism can be said to have ended.
He stands there, flushed and starlit before the mirror,
uttering cryptic phrases, for instance, 'The well
is fed by a spring on the highest point of the island'
and the reflection laughs back with Arcturus
studding the bare shoulder. The finest of all
influences is memory. Zophar, the third
of Job's comforters, says of the secrets of wisdom
that they are double to that which is.
A new enigma is detected gliding
under the surface of words where dark alders
hang low and insects form a dancing cloud.
There are times when no phoenix rises screeching
from its charred nest and the day leads dry
and unconsoling in every direction.
In exile however he gets up early,
breakfasts alone by the sunny window and watches
the lines of snow-capped peaks above the pine-trees
forming the frontier, for here they speak a different language.
He spends each morning at work on his masterpiece.
His hosts are considerate – he has this house
rent-free plus an income. And he is at liberty.
At evening, alone, a sense of pointlessness
enfolds him like smoke. Why pin any hope on the next
generation or on the next but two?

Those who might find these pages scorched with his indignation
of interest, even of use, are distant and timorous.
Sales of his work in translation grow less every year.
He was once a wonder, his books, his integrity
valuable fodder for speeches on freedom
but now it's the tenth day and the world has changed.
This cool gallery is lined with ancestors
of a total stranger, some in armour, some in orange velvet,
proud or stupid or handsome, having one thing in common,
the gift of death. To pass dutifully before each portrait
is little good. One is sometimes in too much of a hurry
even to examine the curl of a peony,
the gleam of light on a far pond or the cloud
whose summer brightness holds a dark blur of rain.
A glint of silver among the shadows of rosewood
recalled that room, do you remember? and the sunset
lighting the end of the street while the high gulls
drifted. The questioner remains austere
in the very centre of recollection. Logic
must never be ignored but cannot equal
conviction like a radiance behind the eyelid.
At rare moments of revelation there is only
the state of being as foliage is in gold air.
I know because I can't be sure, I am aware
but locked in rings of iridescence that conceal
time. There are two kingdoms. You belong in both, the one
where you degenerate and where all paths
must peter out in grass or stone or other paths
and the other where the moment stands
weightless in splendour. The platform was empty.
Milk churns were stacked in the warm shadow.
A smell of haycocks came from the near field

and a score of caged pigeons waited murmuring
for their release. When evening comes you sit
reading and the book falls to your lap and the corn
left by the harvesters sways with ripeness.
Or I watch you sleeping. Every frontier
is made up of such moments. It is a question
never of place but of time. The mirror as well
holds danger especially when, fringed with dusk,
a white face flickers behind you, vanishes.
The future too has barriers between room and room
but at times it is enough to write letters
as the moon's course slants across the square of window
and offer a few friends who may never read them
the chance of sharing in a borrowed midnight.

The Fifth Elegy

Airs of summer wind their way through the empty chamber
for the skulls have gone to stare behind glass at a crude
map on the museum wall. Perhaps the bones
were removed piecemeal when the mound fell in. The sun is low
and slopes of tough grass fleeced with hazel
repeat the fragrance of the day. High stone slabs
freed from burial by five thousand years of rain
stand in the light and frost. You do not like these journeys.
Along a green-sided estuary where the tides race
hedgerows are twined with dogrose and stunted
apple-trees crowd against the white-washed farmhouse.
Fuchsia blooms by the gate until late November.
Beyond the water, fields lift towards the sunset where bare rocks
are whipped by the fog. The ferry would take us dryshod
past a brown seagull floating. The brasswork shines,
flush with the fine red wood. Each screw is countersunk.
Blue leather cushions are spotless and the rowlocks
turn silently. Art matters as itself, as structure,
as joy in its own structure though the function
may be to get something across. You must remain
conscious of the surface, its music, the promise
of another world even when the devil is muttering
lacklustre words. The worst is to be tempted not to try.
Better to scoff forbidden fruit than offer
the easel for sale. You can't make money the way
you make a sonata, make a field give grain,
make love, unless the coins are counterfeit.
The unimportant aspects last each day
from nine to five. It was a still June evening.

The guests stood by the open window. When they'd gone in
to dinner, glancing round the table, she asked
my cousin where the grey lady had gone, the one
all by herself in the other room. And her host warned her
by kicking her under the table for the grey
lady was seldom seen indoors, preferring it seemed
narrow paths of the garden, the scent of stocks
and warm brown bees working among the lavender.
Old houses like churches find it hard to exclude
the bruises of memory and layers of atmosphere
placed there by prayer or perhaps incidentally
because of a quarrel never properly made up –
year after year some grudge against destiny,
letters unsealed that glowed with stale
impressions from abroad. You'll find a lace fan
and a jigsaw in that cabinet – also
a pack of cards with the nines missing. Sculling
on a foreign lake the son who'd sold the estate
heard distinctly the stable-clock chiming. There's a green
cul-de-sac lined with the graves of dogs. The hill
looks over glittering beech-trees to the moor.
You climbed a different path, one that seemed easier,
and we met by a bed of yellow roses
twisted by the wind. The children were there already
pretending to be horses. We saw the white half-moon
and the distant colours of the sea. Naturalism
is an outmoded form. For a millennium
those who were buried in the shadow of that church-tower
have known of life what we know, that reason
reaches only so far before the truth
takes over. Listen now to the first birdcall
as the trees show a barely perceptible

shiver of green. And water too is sacred in well
and trough and font like hawthorn-leaves and the red
cord that links the child to the mother. You struggled
slipping on greasy chalk in the lane that autumn
and your beauty, flushed, laughing, was such that my heart
was seized with more love than I had imagined possible.
Who though can put a face on words or claim
to interpret the sundial? All we can say for certain is
there was a house, a tomb, a copse, and beyond
the land sloped to the river-mouth. This journey
will take its place among the many ways
of identifying movement. The portraits have arrived.
So have your books. Look at the distance. It has been
a cold summer. I was told in the village this morning
that the old man who rowed the ferry has died.
We could hire a car and drive inland to the bridge.
It's not on this map but would you like to go?

The Sixth Elegy

The track, cut in the yellow stone, runs straight
between flowering shrubs. To the left the ground drops,
the trickle of a stream is clearly audible. The southern sky
is hidden by the slope of trees, green upon green,
swaying. On the path it's still, sheltered from the wind.
In one room only, though at frequent intervals,
the furniture was shifted, usually at night,
but not always. This is a fairly well-known
phenomenon – like the spare needles
twisted out of shape inside the sewing-machine
or the pair of scissors found in the empty scullery
with a black zigzag running the length of one blade.
The horse was discovered kicking, terrified,
in a disused room with a door so narrow
they had to break down a wall to get him out.
Puberty seems to provide a focus for these storms
almost as if the child hitherto controlled
by other forces trembles between two
contradictory poles. One often uses 'it"
for a child and perhaps absolute possession
of gender, fixing the young man or woman,
atrophies other powers. What was glimpsed, once, no longer,
between the fickle leaves? A king and queen,
their naked bodies the colour of wild flowers,
stroll laughing and the sound of their laughter
is shrill, anarchic. A fairy huntsman pursues
the unwitting adult and transfixes his head
with a silver lance that vanishes. A tall figure
created itself out of dancing shadows and moved

across the wood like details of another wood.
The house shook slightly. If you treat the symbol
as a screen before an object claiming the thorn
indicates protection or the ruined barn
the failure of the old ideas you reduce the painting
to a work in code. The hills of allegory are real
hills, stars burn and the lion stalks among high trees
lashing its tail. It is often an effort
to look north and south among the images
and those who translate the poem into prose
are praised for having found the solution
for the achievements of intellect are the ones
that seem to count. Lip-service paid to dead poets
or to the statements of religion is as much as most
are prepared to pay. But Blake not alone knew
it's the other way round. What the narrow-minded
conceive of as reality is only the first step.
We have lived elsewhere. How otherwise explain
the shock of recognition at the gap in the hedge,
that day high on the downs when the sun led you
to a place you knew though it was your first visit.
Each dawn renews our loss. Half-creatures, stumbling,
seeing through a divided eye, we slip
from plane to plane and walk bewildered as the light
rises and shifts the distances round until
we are uncertain of our whereabouts and wonder
which one is our companion, which the ghost.
The cuckoo flew hooting above the rowan-tree
where the stone avenue points downhill to the spring
that trickles from the grass. You have seen this
and gone over marshy ground in winter to find
the last brooklime unshrivelled and the crow's

shadow on a litter of bones. The danger
lies not in loneliness but in absorption
leading to self-absorption. This was never meant.
There is the need to be kissed and the need
to be by oneself. Our children called out in sleep
and my own nightmare put the wrong faces on friends.
No comfort issues from the dark. There is a splendour
inside the heart that cannot be challenged.
Who is that pale woman with grey hair standing
silent in the white room? She smiles as though
she recognised who we are. The moat is frozen,
the orchard stark and bare. If we are patient
there won't be time for questions at the end.